LET'S TOON!

CARICATURES

BY KEELAN PARHAM

CARICATURES

LET'S TOON!

Published By Lunar Donut Press/FL

To Barbie, Brady and Kaley, "my girls".

Text, art, "Let's Toon" and "PENN", are © 2003, 2007, 2009 by Keelan Parham

Published by Lunar Donut Press,
PO Box 692625, Orlando,FL, 32869
www.lunardonut.com
www.keelanparham.com
www.caricatureconnection.com

Library of Congress Card Number: 2002095936
ISBN 0-9725638-0-6

Printed in the United States of America

Third printing, 2009

CONTENTS

ACKNOWLEDGEMENTS

I am grateful to so many people who, to varying degrees, made this book possible. Foremost among them: my beautiful wife Barbie (for hanging the moon and making my life so incredible), my daughters, Brady & Kaley (my inspirations), Mom and Dad (for always encouraging me to draw), my sister Lorie (for her love and support), and Ted Tucker (for being my best friend and the brother I never had).

I also want to thank Johnny for his computer talents, Barbie for her photography expertise, and most of all, my Lord Jesus Christ, for making all of this possible. (I figured I'd better get that in there while I could, since my chances of getting to make an acceptance speech at the Grammy Awards are pretty slim!).

Finally, special thanks goes out to: all the artists of Caricature Connection, all the models who graciously posed for this book, all my friends in the National Caricaturists Network, and to all the people I've had the pleasure of drawing over the last fifteen years. Thanks for being so funny looking! May God bless you all!

INTRODUCTION

In this, my first book on cartooning, I've decided to tackle a subject very near and dear to my heart; Caricatures. For the past ten years, I've spent the majority of my waking hours drawing them. I've drawn over 300,000 caricatures in that amount of time...that's a lot of faces! And to this day, with each drawing I do, I feel like I learn something new about the art, and about the human face.

Over the years, without a doubt the most common question I've been asked as a caricature artist is, "Where did you learn to do this?" To be honest, I still don't have an answer for that! I know it wasn't in art school. They didn't even encourage cartooning, much less caricatures. I know it wasn't in books, because back then I couldn't find any on the subject. Lastly, I was never trained in drawing them by anyone I worked with either.

Truthfully, I learned how to draw caricatures by actually getting a job drawing them, and needing money to eat! Hunger is a great motivator, and as we've all heard, necessity is the mother of invention. I vividly remember my first week on the job, and how terrified I was. So much so, that I just stood against the wall of the stand where I worked with another artist, and watched her draw. For the entire week! Finally, I had watched her long enough, and "stolen" enough of her tricks of the trade, that I drew my first caricature. I wish I could say it was a great work of art, but it wasn't. But the model liked it, so that was good enough. That was how my learning of caricatures began. Over the years, each time I saw an artist doing something I liked, I'd try to do my version of it. Whether it was someone I worked with, or someone whose work I saw in a book or magazine, I'd try to combine the things I liked about their work with my other influences (cartoons and comic books) and my own style. What resulted was how I draw caricatures today.

When my wife and I eventually started our own caricature company, Caricature Connection, I began to offer training to the artists who worked with me. It didn't take me long to realize that each time I helped a new artist, I had to repeat the same things, and draw the same examples, over and over again. So, I began putting together an instruction manual that I could just hand out to everyone. What you hold in your hands is what that manual, over the years, has become. I hope you'll find this book informative and entertaining, and when someone asks you how YOU learned to draw caricatures so well, I'd be honored to think that you might name my book as one of your influences!

I could go into the history of caricature here, which is one of my favorite subjects, but that's not what this book is about. What it is about is learning to draw caricatures, and having fun with them. Drawing caricatures is all about seeing. It's your interpretation of the person's face. From the style you use, the degree of exaggeration you use, all the way to the medium you use, you're in control!

Finally, let me add that the best thing a caricaturist can do, or any artist for that matter, is to look at the works of their fellow artists. There are so many good caricaturists working today, and so many masters of the form who are no longer with us. Look at the work of Al Hirschfeld, Miguel Covarrubias, Al Frueh, Mort Drucker, and Sebastian Kruger, just to name a very few. Try to figure out how and why they interpreted things the way they did. Immerse yourself in their works, and practice, practice, practice!

And most of all... Have Fun!

Keelan Parham

1) Black marker (Permanent ink if you'll be coloring with a wet medium like watercolor.)
2) Sketchbook or even laser paper (For finished pieces, I use 110 lb card stock or Bristol.)
3) A #2 pencil (I used a black colored pencil for some of the shading in this book.)
4) Eraser (Even the best artists need one!)

CARICATURE

...is: "the ludicrous exaggeration of the characteristic features of a subject."

So when you see big stuff, like Mikey's eyes...

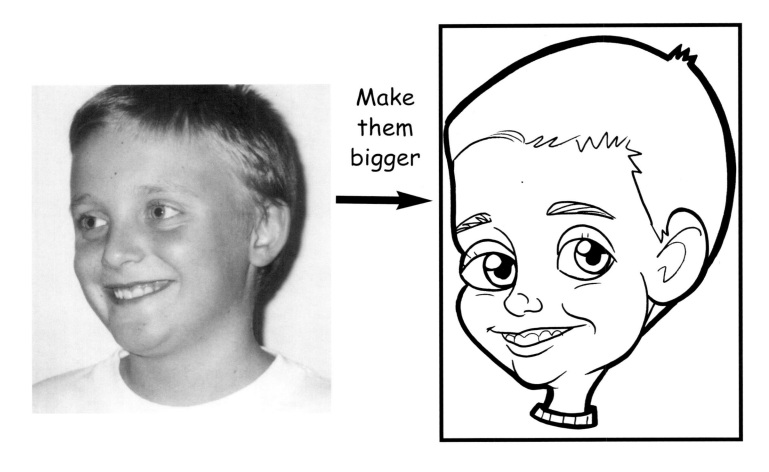

Make them bigger

Then, when you see small stuff, like Rafael's eyes...

...make them smaller!

The same goes for anything you see on a face: round things should be drawn rounder, angular things should be drawn more angular, long things should be drawn longer, short things should be drawn shorter, etc. Whatever you see exaggerate it!

First, look at your model, interpret them through your own artistic vision, and then put that onto the paper. It's easy, right? Too many people try to make caricaturing too difficult!

PENN'S TIP:

People tend to think a caricature highlights your <u>worst</u> features. This isn't actually correct. Caricatures highlight your most <u>distinctive</u> features. In other words, what makes you look like <u>YOU</u>!!!

INTRODUCING..."NORM"!

In caricaturing, we draw an exaggerated, cartoon version of the face. But before we start learning to exaggerate, we first need to understand the average, or normal measurements of the face. Let's start with a drawing of a fellow we'll call Norm, since his face gives us the "Normal" guidelines for all faces:

The width of Norm's face is four to five of his eye-widths across.

His eyes are one eye width apart. (This is true in 3/4 views as well!)

His nose is two eye widths long.

From the tip of his nose to the bottom of his upper lip is one eye width long.

The corners of Norm's mouth line up with the center of his eyes.

The top of his ears line up with his eyebrows.

Now that we've established the "Normal" facial measurements, we just keep them in mind as we draw other, real faces.

In other words, when a model sits down for you to draw, you ask yourself, "Is his nose longer or shorter than 'Norm's'?" "Are his eyes closer together or farther apart?"

14

How much you exaggerate faces, and what style you draw them in, is up to you. Let's see what we can do here with Ted:

I could draw him like this, which is fairly tame...

..or, I could draw him a bit more exaggerated, like this...

Keep in mind when exaggerating, you run the risk of insulting your model! People usually (but not always) know physical flaws they have, and may not be happy if you exaggerate those flaws! It is rare to find a person that has a sense of humor about his or her own appearance.

...Or, I could go really simple and cartoony and draw Ted like this...

...Or, I could even go abstract with him...

It's up to you! You're the artist and can decide what style you work in on each drawing! You'll notice in this book that I use a number of styles myself! Experiment and have fun!

PENN'S TIP:

Don't be fooled! Drawing in a "simple" style is really more difficult! With details, you can always "dress up" a drawing and have something to "hide behind", to cover up its flaws. If you go simple, you'd better have it right! The important thing to remember about whatever style you use though is to be consistent with it! For example, if you put a detailed body on a simple face, it obviously won't match!

SETTING UP

Whether you're drawing from a photo or from a live model, one of the most important things you can do as an artist is to make sure you're at the proper viewing distance and position to your model. I always hold the photo, like the one of Diane here, as close as possible to the paper I'm drawing on. This allows me to see almost an "after image" of the photo on my paper. My eyes go back and forth, from the photo to the paper, making sure I've drawn each feature correctly.

PENN'S TIP:

Photos tend to "flatten out" the face somewhat, being two-dimensional. Lighting also can be a problem. It is best to get multiple photos with different views of the face and look at each of them as you draw. Also, try to make sure the face in the photo is at least as big as a dime, so you can see the features well.

If you decide to draw live, at parties or at retail venues, like I have for so many years, your position in relation to your model is even more important.

Some artists like their models right up next to them:

While other artists like their models slightly farther away:

Personally, I like my models 4-5 feet away from my easel. I find it "blurs out" some of the extraneous details and helps me concentrate on what's important about the features. Sometimes I even squint my eyes as I look at the model to accomplish the same thing.

Another trick I use in setting up is putting the model almost "behind" the easel, no matter how far away they are sitting. Here's what this looks like from the artist's position:

Again, just like with a photo, what you're after is getting as little distance as possible for your eyes to travel from the model's face to the drawing surface. The more distance your eyes have to travel, the more chance there is to lose "mental information" about their face. This often results in a caricature with a very poor, or no likeness.

PENN'S TIP:

All of the illustrations in this book are drawn from a right-hander's orientation. If you're a "lefty", put your model on the other side of your easel and face them to the right. You'll find it easier...trust me!

VIEWS AND SEQUENCING

When drawing from a photo, you don't have a choice as to which view of your model, full face, three quarter, or profile, you will draw. When drawing live, however, it's the first important decision you will make. Look at the person's features and decide which view of their face will make the drawing look most like them. For example, for someone with a big nose, draw a profile. With a model that has big ears, choose a front view.

Spectators and beginning caricaturists often ask, "How do you know what to draw next?" In my studio work, I usually start with the head shape. In my live work, however, I keep the head

shape in mind but start with the features, drawing left to right across the face. Having a method like this is called "sequencing". On the following pages, I show you the sequencing that I recommend for each view. But truthfully it doesn't matter where you start (heck, start with the nose hairs, if you want) as long as it looks like the person! Now at this point in the book we haven't covered each of the individual features and how to draw them, but we will soon. Before we go any further, we need to decide what view we're going to draw, and the sequencing:

FRONT VIEW

The advantage here is that people are used to seeing themselves from this view. The disadvantage is that it can be difficult to line up the sides of the face to make them even.

①

Left eye

②

Bridge of nose, right eye

③

Left eyebrow, right eyebrow, more nose bridge

④

Tip of nose

⑤

Upper lip, corners of mouth

⑥

Teeth, bottom lip

⑦

Chin

⑧

Left side of face,
then right side

⑨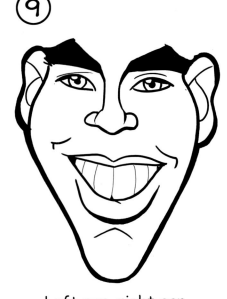

Left ear, right ear

⑩

Inside shape of hair

⑪

Outside shape of
hair and blacking in

⑫

Detailing, like
dimples, smile lines,
etc. Voila!

3/4 VIEW

This is the view I use the most in "live" caricaturing. I find it is also the easiest to learn. The reason for this is it makes the shape of the forehead, cheekbones and bridge of the nose particularly visible.

 ①

Left eye

②

Ridge above the eye

③

Left eyebrow, left side of nose bridge

④

Right side of nose bridge, right eyebrow

⑤

Right eye, rest of nose

⑥

Upper lip, front left to right, right smile line

PENN'S TIP:

The sequencing we have shown is from a right-handed artist's perspective. For "lefty" artists, turn the model the opposite direction.

⑦

Teeth, lower lip, and chin

⑧

Left cheek, left smile line, left side of forehead

⑨

Starting in center of forehead, draw the main stroke of the inside hair contour, then the outside

⑩

Finish right side of hair, then left side of hair, from top to bottom

⑪

Complete right side of jaw, neck and shoulders, ends of hair

⑫

Details in hair and face

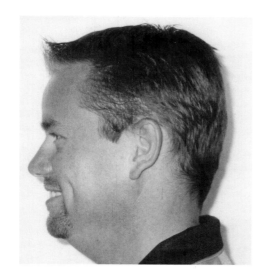

SIDE VIEW (PROFILE)

The advantage here is that it's quick, since you only have to draw half the face! But be warned...no one sees their profile naturally (except in a photo), so there is more of a tendency for your model to say "That doesn't look like me!" even when it obviously does.

①

Bridge of nose down to the tip, the side and nostril

②

Upper lip

③

Teeth line

④

Bottom lip

⑤

Chin and front neck line

⑥

Cheek line

25

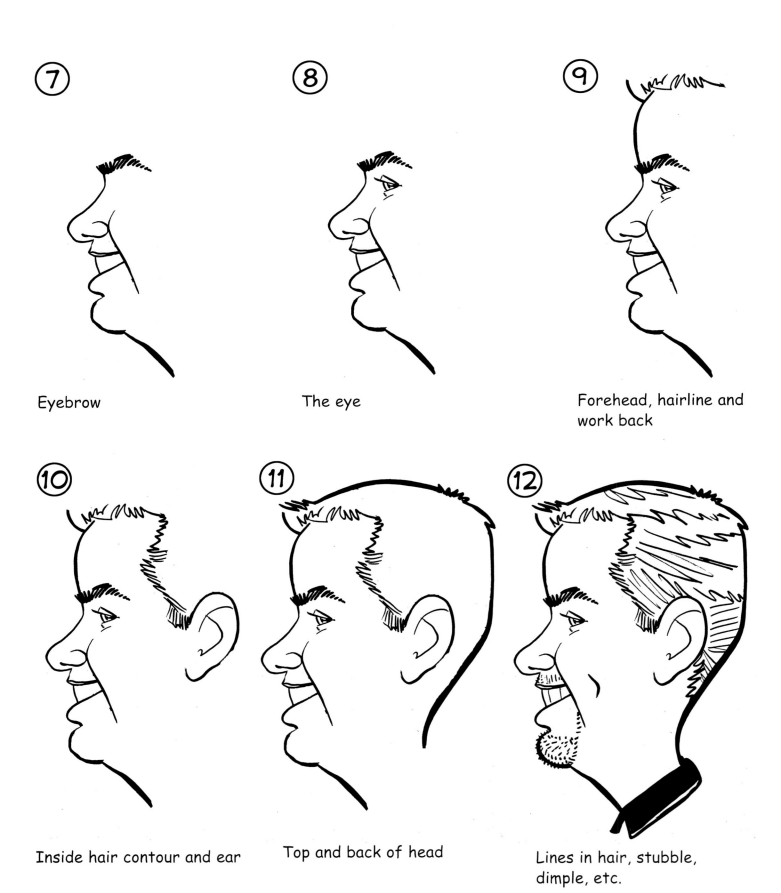

⑦ Eyebrow

⑧ The eye

⑨ Forehead, hairline and work back

⑩ Inside hair contour and ear

⑪ Top and back of head

⑫ Lines in hair, stubble, dimple, etc.

EVERYBODY'S FACE IS DIFFERENT, SO PAY ATTENTION TO THE GENERAL DIRECTION OF THEIR PROFILE! IT'LL USUALLY FALL INTO ONE OF THESE CATEGORIES:

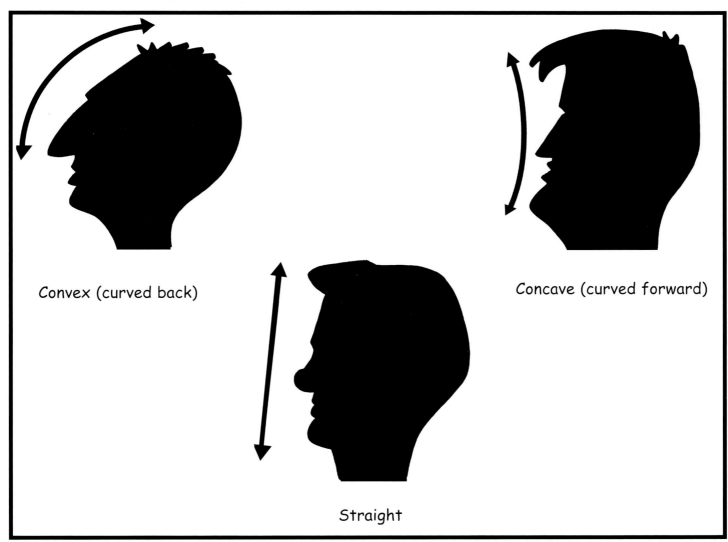

Convex (curved back)

Concave (curved forward)

Straight

FACE SHAPES

The face shape is the first feature you should look at on someone you're about to draw. This is really the single most important thing you have to determine in order to make your drawing look like your model.

The basic face shapes of people are pretty simple. In fact, I bet you'll recognize them:

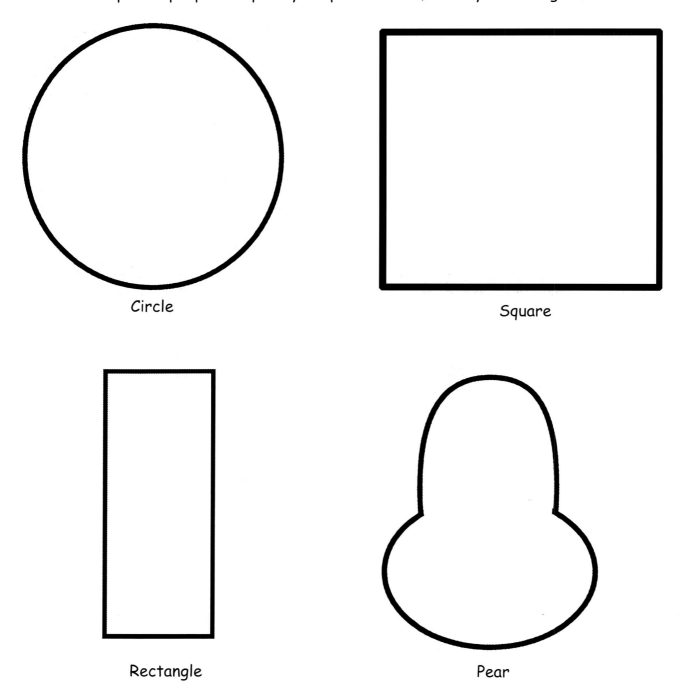

Circle

Square

Rectangle

Pear

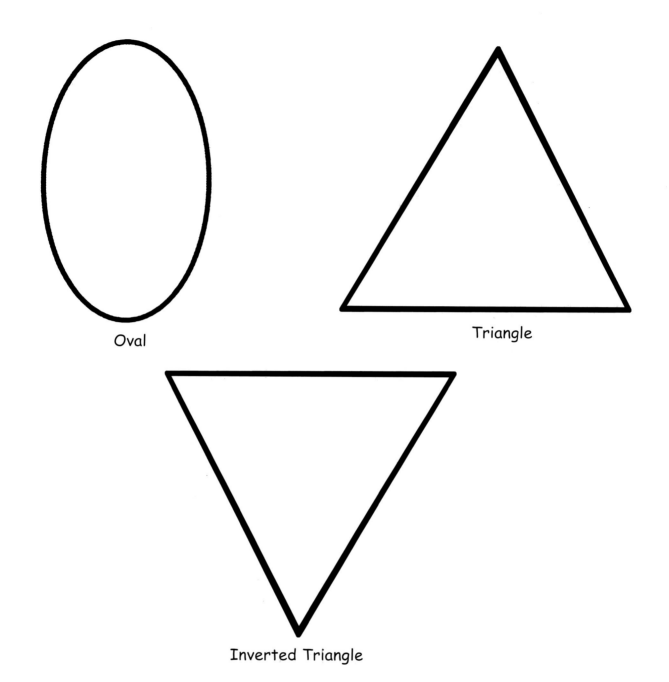

Oval

Triangle

Inverted Triangle

These are just the basics. You can also vary them slightly and see that some people even have diamond or heart shaped heads, to name a few more. But few people's face shapes are as definite as any of these, not when you add skin, fat, chins, ears, noses, etc. Look closely, and you should be able to determine the shape pretty easily.

PENN'S TIP:

Once you determine your model's face shape, keep it in mind as you draw, no matter what view you use!

Let me give you an example.

When I looked at Marion, I saw a rectangular shape to his face and decided that drawing the front view would best show this. Next I notice that his forehead is small, and his eyebrows thick and wiry. His lips are very defined for a man and his mouth turns up at the corners. This gives him a perpetually happy look. So my drawing of him came out like this:

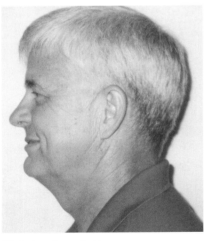

Think about it...you can recognize your best friend or a family member a whole block away, right? Why is that? What is it about people you know that makes them recognizable to you, even at a distance? It can't be their eye color or the freckle on their cheek because you can't see those things at a distance. So, what CAN you see? The relation of their features to each other, their body language, and you know it's coming...their face shape!

30

What do you notice on this model, Monica?

Her face is also rectangular, but her cheeks make it curve out on the sides. Her chin recedes into her neck in the front view. Her smile shows upper teeth and tongue, and in the front view, a hint of her bottom teeth.

PENN'S TIP:

Ask yourself as you're drawing your model, What is absolutely essential to their 'look'?" THAT'S the thing or things that you have to make sure you depict correctly. Anything else is just unneeded detail! **WHEN IN DOUBT LEAVE IT OUT!**

Now we'll look at Dion:

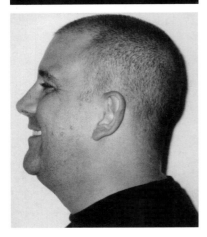

When I went to draw him, I saw a pear shape to his head. I also noticed his squinty eyes, double chin and large ears. But, my eyes kept coming back to the head shape, so I decided on a simpler, more abstract approach. By "pushing" or exaggerating the pear shape even more, it became a figure eight, so my drawing ended up like this:

With Jeanie I saw: an oval face, high forehead, prominent sides to her jaw, wide smile, eyes that droop ever so slightly at the corners, and heavy eyelids.

The first thing I noticed about Johnny was the strong oval shape to his head (It's almost perfectly round). Secondly, I noticed his nose points up a bit. I also saw that his eyes slant down on the ends, and his ears are tilted in at the top and out at the bottom. His chin is also much narrower than the top of his head, reinforcing my observation of his head being an oval. So, here's my drawing:

Tammy has a square jaw, incredible dimples, one eye slightly larger than the other, and a smile that is higher on her left than her right.

Often when you look at a face, you'll notice that features on one side of it don't perfectly match up with the other side. This is an important concept called **ASYMMETRY**. Look at everyone in this book, and at your friends and family. They all have some asymmetry to their faces! It's things like asymmetry, all those little imperfections, that make each face unique and beautiful in its own way. Perfect is boring!

33

Next, let's try something really tricky and look at two faces that are very similar, twins in fact, and see if we can still pick out the differences. Daniel is on the top and Manuel is on the bottom:

Upon first glance they look almost identical. But I noticed Daniel's face is wide, while Manuel's is long. Manuel's nose is more pointed and Daniel's smile shows both his upper and lower teeth. The slightly different hairstyles helped out as well. So my drawings came out like this:

Pay close attention when drawing twins and you'll usually be able to pick out the differences between them. It's rare, but I have drawn twins that truly were identical. In that case, I'll have one smile with teeth, and the other without, or draw one full face and the other in a three quarter view. I'll do anything to make them look slightly different. This is also a technique I use with siblings who aren't twins, but just look a lot alike.

EXAGGERATION

What if we want to exaggerate the face a little bit more? That is, after all, one of the main things people think about when they think about caricatures. How do you do it? And what do you exaggerate?

What stands out about Michael? To me it's his oval head that's narrower at the top, his thinning hairline, his large forehead, his eyes with their smile lines, his nose shape, his mouth shape (thin lips), the shapes of his teeth, and his ears.

So now I know <u>what</u> to exaggerate, but I still need to know how.

The main principle of exaggeration is:

"SQUASH AND STRETCH"

In other words, if you squash an object in one place, you have to equally stretch it in another place, and vice versa.

To illustrate, think of the face as being printed on a piece of rubber:

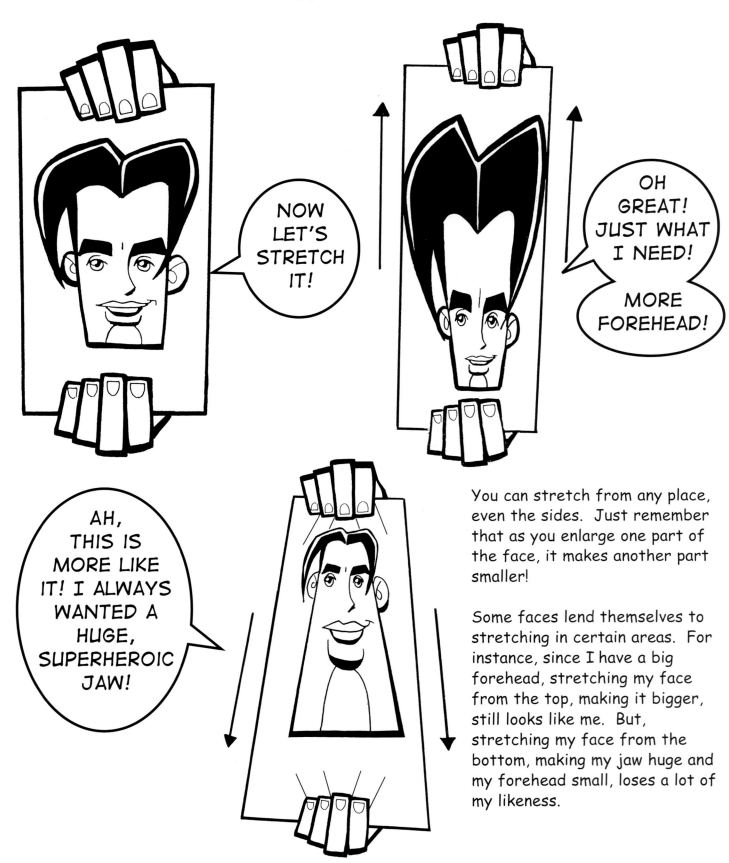

NOW LET'S STRETCH IT!

OH GREAT! JUST WHAT I NEED!

MORE FOREHEAD!

AH, THIS IS MORE LIKE IT! I ALWAYS WANTED A HUGE, SUPERHEROIC JAW!

You can stretch from any place, even the sides. Just remember that as you enlarge one part of the face, it makes another part smaller!

Some faces lend themselves to stretching in certain areas. For instance, since I have a big forehead, stretching my face from the top, making it bigger, still looks like me. But, stretching my face from the bottom, making my jaw huge and my forehead small, loses a lot of my likeness.

36

When I tried this on Michael, I looked at all three of his photos, but stuck with the full-face view. My reason for this was even though the three quarter view also showed the face shape really well, I felt his ears were very important to his "look", and the front view showed them the best.

The more I looked at his face, I realized I could actually push & pull it into a diamond shape, and came up with this:

Over the next few pages, I'll show you some more faces, some of which I've exaggerated more, and some less:

Alex:

Oval (but almost upside down triangle face) + ears that angle out + large pupils in eyes =

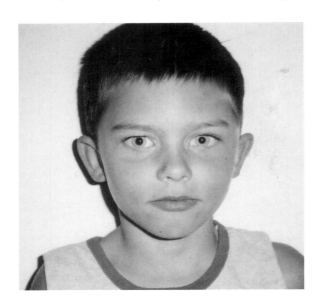 

Lilly Ann:

Square face + eyes that are slightly different size + only half visible eyebrow on one side + wide nose tip + lack of prominent chin =

Doug:

Inverted triangle head (bigger at top than bottom) + high forehead + lively eyes + distinctive hair + lots of perfect teeth + prominent gums =

Kelsey:

Rectangular head + high forehead + pretty eyes + upturned nose + crowded teeth =

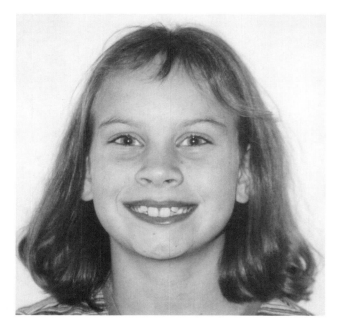

John:

Square face + wiry hair + wide nose + large distance from nose to lips + friendly, small smile + large ears =

Stephanie:

Rectangle face + distinctive hairstyle + arched eyebrows + glasses =

AGES

What makes one person look older than another and how do we draw that? Let's start by looking at Marco and his son, Marc, and comparing their faces:

 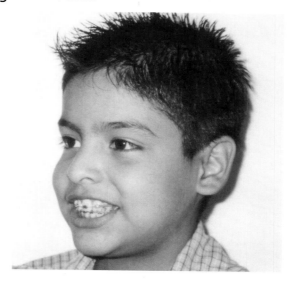

You see in Marc's photo that children usually have:
1) Larger eyes   2) Softer features (fewer angles or hard lines)   3) Less of a definite nose structure   4) Less prominent chin   5) Thinner eyebrows   6) Larger ears
7) More head above their eyes than below

Now let's see my drawings of these guys:

This time, let's look at Laura and her daughter, Jordan:

You see pretty much the same differences as in the guys' photos, right?

Remember these differences and use them to your advantage! Occasionally you may have to draw a child who doesn't look very "child-like"; the little boy who looks like a miniature man, or the ten-year-old girl who looks fifteen. In these cases, I really use my "young tricks" to full advantage. I enlarge the eyes, shorten the chin, etc.

Finally, let's compare a young person and an elderly person. Here's Adelene, and her granddaughter, Erin:

A lot of the differences we previously outlined are still present, but some of them have changed places. Now the older person has the thinner eyebrows, the less prominent chin and larger ears!

So we see that as they get older, in many ways, faces regress to qualities they had when they were very young! As faces age, some features become more defined, and some less.

In looking at these photos of Joanie and David...

...**We see things to look for in the faces of "Senior" models:** **1)** Smaller eyes
2) Thinner eyebrows **3)** Larger ears **4)** More prominent noses **5)** Wrinkles **6)** Looser skin
7) Thinner hair

PENN'S TIP:

With older models don't get carried away with the wrinkles! Drawing a lot of lines in the face can really clutter up the clean, cartoony style we're after. As always, only put in what's necessary to get their "look'!

EYES

Now that we've started learning what to look for in faces, let's take each feature and learn how to draw it. The eyes can indicate emotions, attitude, personality, age and even race. So, how do we draw a good cartoon/caricature eye? Well, as you'll see as you look through this book I use all different kinds!

In my experience, people really seem to like this kind of eye:

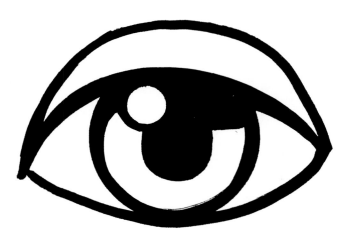

Or, what I call the "animation eye", as it's used on most of the human characters in today's television and feature animation.

Draw a "football shape".

Add a circle. This is going to be our eyeball.

Make a black dot for the pupil. This should always be in the exact center of your eyeball.

Add a small circle to the upper left of the pupil. This is our "highlight".

Draw in the shadow created by the upper eyelid.

Add the upper eyelid itself, and any final details, like eyelashes. Ta-da!!! A great cartoon eye!

46

Here it is in action:

Not everyone has light colored eyes, like Gail does. Below we see Tisha with her big brown eyes. When I'm drawing in color, I draw darker eyes, the same way I do light ones and just color them in. In black & white, I usually draw them as all black with a highlight like this:

PENN'S TIP:

The model here is Asian, so her eye shape is a little different than those of the other models in this book. God made such wonderful differences among the different races, you should pay attention to them when drawing!

You can even choose to simplify the dark eye further by dropping out the white around it altogether, like I did on Dillon here:

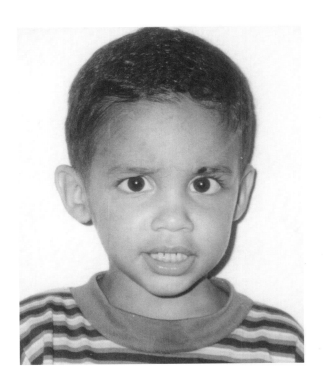 

And on Dylan here:

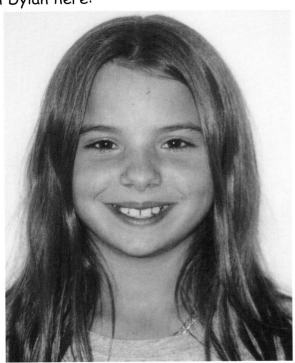 

Obviously with boys and men, the more eyelashes you draw on them and the more prominent you make them, the more feminine your model will look. So be careful and don't overdo it!

EYE DIRECTION

You'll notice that in all of my drawings, even the three quarter and profile views, I make the model look out at us, regardless of what they're doing in their photo. My reason? I'll show you by example:

In the top photo of Barry, which is a front view, notice how he's looking out at us. But in the three quarter photo under it, notice how detached he looks, looking away from us. So in my drawing of this view, I turned his eyes toward us, the viewers. See how it makes more of a "connection" with us this way?

Because he is looking at us now, notice how much more friendly and inviting the drawing is. Remember, people like friendly drawings!

In live caricaturing, I try to have the model look off, past me, rather than into my eyes. With a full-face view, I have them look out over my left shoulder, that way we're not "staring each other down".

Some people, like Mike here, just aren't comfortable posing for drawings or photos. If they feel they're being stared at, it can make them feel even more uncomfortable.

When I first started drawing live caricatures I would become flustered when I'd have to draw those huge football-loving guys who I just knew had been beaten or bribed to sit for a drawing. They'd just stare at me with an "I'm going to eat you for lunch" look on their faces, or at least that's how I perceived it! I think that's the reason I drew only three quarter views for years, so I wasn't being stared at. Now I've come to realize they were probably just nervous, and I, being the artist drawing them, intimidated them! Remember, the best drawings result from you AND your model being comfortable!

NOSES

Yeah, I know the old saying: "It's as plain as the nose on your face", but noses really aren't plain! Just look at some of these shapes:

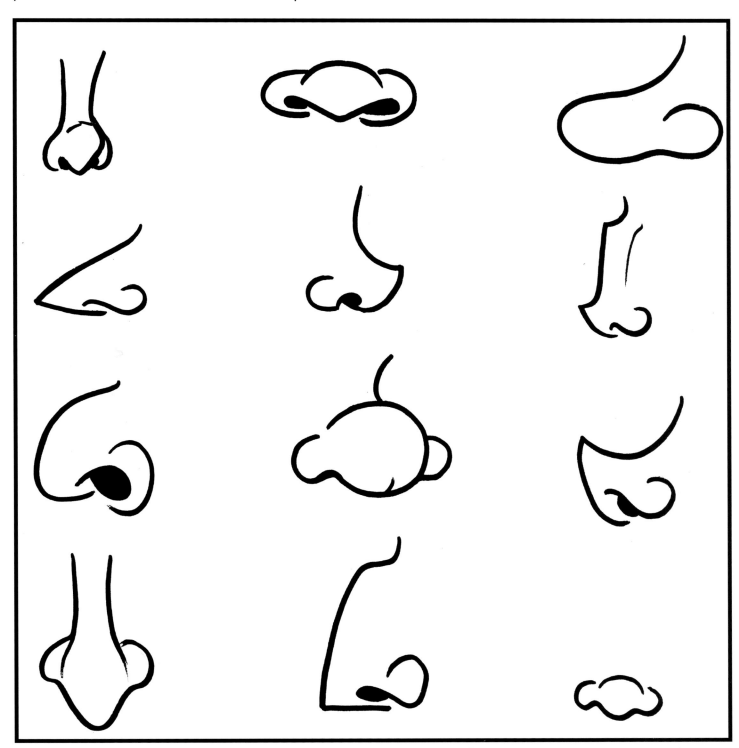

And there are millions more!

Regardless of the actual shape of the nose, it's always made up of the same parts:

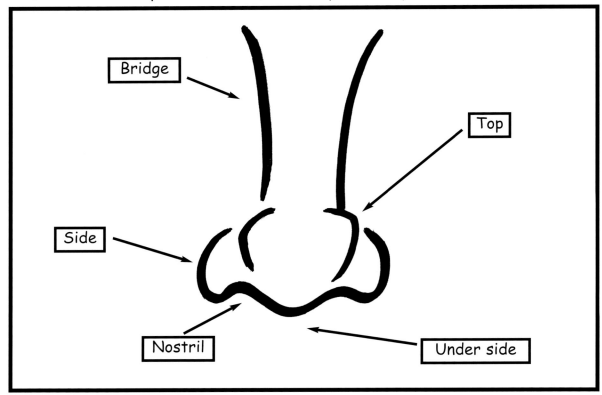

The same nose, 3/4 view, would look like this:

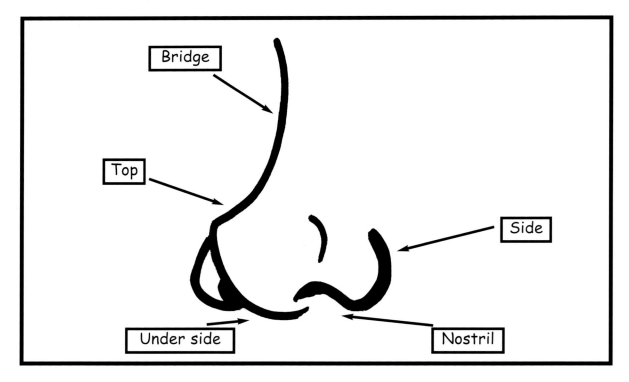

The nose is one of the first features I look at when I start to draw someone. Being in the center of the face, I think it's one of the most important components of a person's likeness.

MOUTHS

On any mouth you draw, all of these parts will be present to some degree:

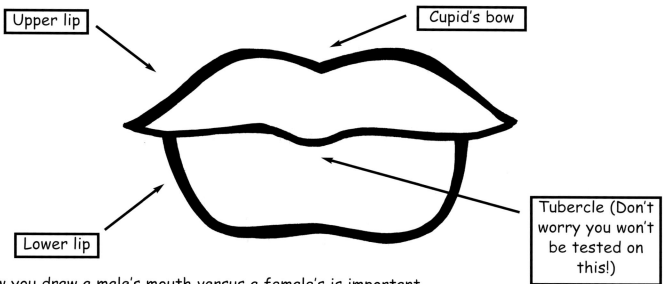

Upper lip

Cupid's bow

Lower lip

Tubercle (Don't worry you won't be tested on this!)

How you draw a male's mouth versus a female's is important.

Q. Which of these mouths belongs to a male and which one belongs to a female?

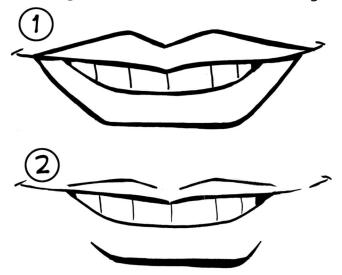

①

②

A. Number one is the female, and number two is the male. How do we know this? They're two very similar mouths, but with a couple of minor differences. To begin with, the second one has a thinner upper lip, since most men's lips aren't as thick as those of women. The other difference is my use of "broken lines" to make the lips more masculine. If your lines are too solid in drawing your mouths, it will make them look feminine. It's a small thing that can make a big difference in your drawings. Many times I've heard boys and men say, upon seeing an artist's drawing, "I look like a girl!" The main reasons for this are solid line, feminine looking lips, and long eyelashes. On males, play down any so-called "feminine" features they may have, and on females, play down any masculine features you see.

TEETH

To teeth or not to teeth...that is the question! In most cases, I think drawing the individual teeth of your model reinforces the likeness. There are such incredible variations in the size, shape, and yes, color, of teeth. But, the first question you need to ask is, "How distinctive are his/her teeth?" or "Are the teeth really an integral part of the person's look?"

Lindsey has such perfect teeth...

...that I just drew her with what I call a "tooth bar", with no indication of individual teeth:

But with Michael...

...I obviously had to draw his teeth in:

For Randy, however, even though his teeth are also perfect, they are very distinctive...

...so much so, that in my abstract style, they're some of the only things I wanted to make sure I included:

Finally, we come to braces. With Reeve as an example, you can see I draw them as simply as possible:

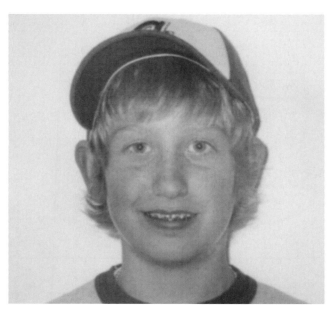

This is so you don't call undue attention to them. One thing people with braces will do is try to smile with their mouth shut, hiding the braces. I try to get them to open up, though, explaining that braces change the entire shape of their mouth, whether or not their mouth is open.

Another mouth subject is gums. Don has very visible gums when he smiles, so I made sure I included them:

Other people, like Shea, for example, may not have visible gums at all when they smile:

PENN'S TIP:

Whenever possible get your model to smile. Think about it - why do we smile in photographs? Because it's generally felt that we look our best when we smile. Smiling also makes you look like you are having fun, and that is one of the biggest elements we want to inject into our caricatures - FUN! Plus, if you're drawing live, when spectators come up and see your model smiling, and their picture smiling, they'll be more inclined to get their own picture drawn!

The exceptions to drawing your models smiling are squirmy babies and someone that rarely smiles.

For example, I don't think I've ever seen Jandi smile very big. So, if I drew her with a big "cheesy" grin, how would she, or anyone else who knows her, recognize her? It wouldn't look like her!

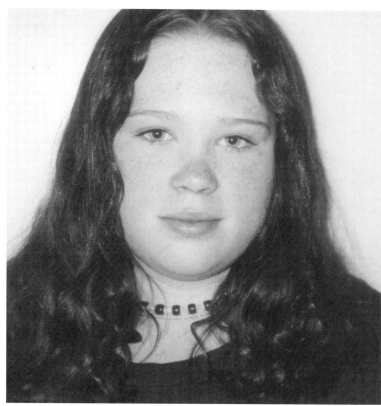

Therefore, I drew her like this:

Remember you want to depict a person's typical look, in order to "nail" the likeness.

When you're drawing smiles, pay close attention. Just look at all the variations in this book alone! There are smiles that:

(1) Show no teeth (like Jandi's here)

(2) Show only a little bit of teeth:

(3) Show only the upper teeth:

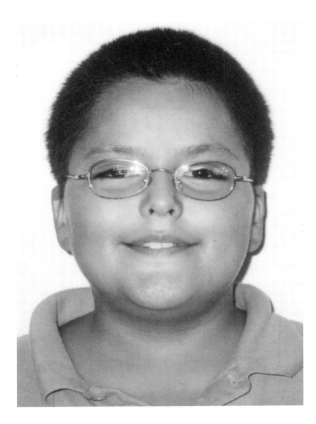

(4) Show upper teeth and tongue:

(5) Show upper teeth and lower teeth:

⑥ Show upper teeth, lower teeth and tongue:

⑦ Smiles that are straight across:

(8) Smiles that turn up:

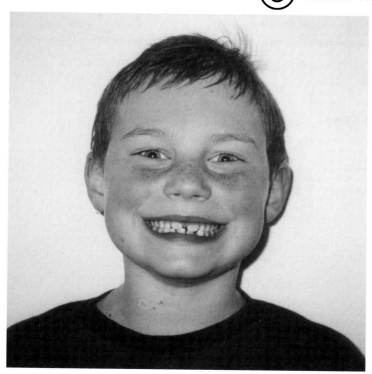 

and (9) Smiles that turn down:

EAR'S TO YA

Just look at all of the twists, spirals, and folds in the ears of your models! No wonder cartoonists simplify them when they draw! Here are some popular ways to do just that:

This one is pretty close to a "real" ear and the one I use a lot and highly recommend.

The "6" ear. As long as the rest of your style fits, feel free to use this kind of visual shorthand! This is the most abstract of the ear designs I use.

The "J" ear. This is a variation of a"6" ear, and a real ear.

This is what I call the "S" ear. No one's ear really looks like this, but remember, we're drawing cartoons!

From the front, one way to draw ears is to make them a variation on a capital "B" shape, then just add the inside loops.

Here's the "B" shape ear on Mike:

Another thing to pay attention to on your models' ears is what angle they're set on the head. Austin's ears, for example, angle out:

So I made sure I drew them that way. And exaggerated them, of course!

63

HAIR

When drawing hair, think of it as shapes, not as individual hairs. Kellie's hairstyle is a perfect example:

Notice the strong rectangular shape, and how it frames her face:

Kathy's hair also has a definite rectangular shape:

You'll also notice I draw the outside lines thicker than the inside lines in order to keep everything neat and clean looking.

Pete here, like Kathy, has an easy hairstyle to draw, right? As I was drawing, I thought of it in three distinct shapes, or sections; the left side, the top, and the right side.

You'll notice though, some "normal" hairstyles, like braids, can be a challenge to draw simply and quickly if you're not used to them. Here's how I handled Anna's braids:

I drew the outside lines of the braids first and then drew the "X" shape on them for a clean, graphic symbol to easily get the point across.

Very curly hair, like Elizabeth's, can also be tricky. I made sure to correctly depict how loose or tight the curls are, and again used thick outside lines and thin inside lines.

When a model has longer hair, like Barbie, I usually lengthen it in my drawing of them:

This is to compensate for how the small body and large head would make the hair look short. Also, it exaggerates the hair length. Remember, caricature is about exaggeration! Another thing I want to point out is how I made the area of her hair around her face darker so it draws attention to her face. This is a trick I often use in my black and white drawings to make them look better.

Many times I have to draw models that have their hair pulled back in some way, like in a ponytail. As you can see in Clarissa's picture, I "cheat" a bit and pull the ponytail to the side a little, so we can see they have more hair:

If you can't draw the hairstyle right away, get the model to turn their head so you can see it from a couple of angles! Looking at Lisa from the side helped me understand her hairstyle so I could better draw it from the front.

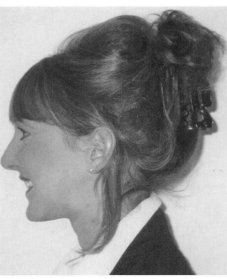

Another thing to do when drawing hair is "cleaning up" the edges and ends of their hair. Here's what I did on Toni:

See? I cleaned up the edges, and took away the "wispies". She'll like the drawing better this way, and the "wispies" wouldn't have been easy to depict accurately since they're of such fine hair. Remember - Simplify! Which is exactly why I chose to draw Jason's hair the way I did here:

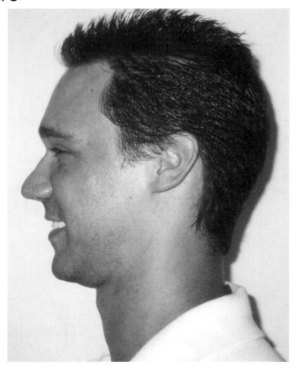 

Drawing his hair as a solid black shape was a quick, easy way to do it.

Sometimes when drawing darker hair, I use black in the shadow areas and leave white for the highlights like Evie's here:

Notice how the lighting is from above, so the top surfaces of the hair receive the light, while the folds and curls are in shadow and remain black!

If I was doing a color drawing, I would then put the appropriate hair color in the white areas.

Lastly, we come to the ...uh..."follically challenged" part of our hair section. With models with little or no hair, remember two important things:

① Be accurate when you draw the shape of the top of the head. Greg's head is very round on top, but some people are relatively flat there or even have a point to their head.

② Include a temple line. In this drawing, the temple line is the one that runs from his left eyebrow up his forehead. This helps give the drawing some depth. Without it, it's difficult to tell where the forehead ends and the side of the head starts.

FACIAL ACCESSORIES

Whether they're temporary or permanent, facial accessories can help complete the likeness.

Permanent features like birthmarks, freckles, moles and scars are all things that can be integral to a likeness. But use sensitivity when drawing them!

The little cutie above, Katie, is always on the move, and always seems to have a bandage somewhere...so I included it in my drawing of her. In a retail setting, however, I would've asked her parents if they'd mind if I put the bandage in the drawing, or prefer I leave it out.

I handle temporary things like acne, bruises, cuts, scratches and mild facial stubble the same way. I ask their opinion before I draw it. The same suggestion I said before, "When in doubt, leave it out!" applies here as well.

An important thing to remember about these accessories is that they are add-ons, and shouldn't get in the way of drawing the most important part of the picture - the likeness. For this reason, when I draw glasses, you'll see that I draw the person's face first, <u>without</u> the glasses. Once I have the likeness correct, I add the glasses. Here's a demonstration on Lucia:

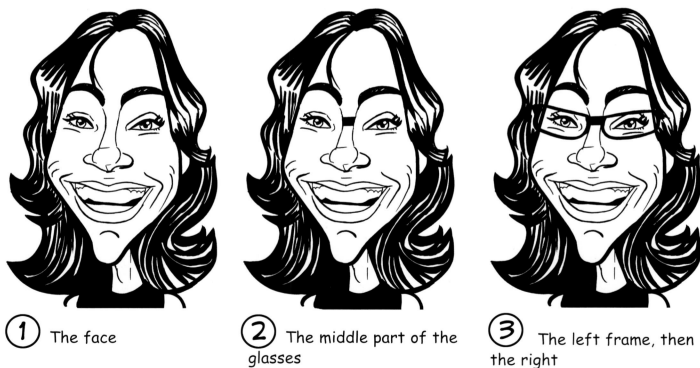

① The face   ② The middle part of the glasses   ③ The left frame, then the right

When drawing the frames, draw them in one continuous motion to make the shape as smooth and clean as possible.

I drew Jason in the same way:

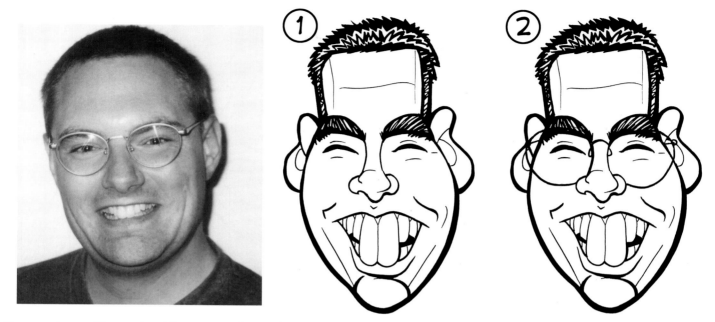

Remember, first the likeness, then the accessories! Here it is on Marshal:

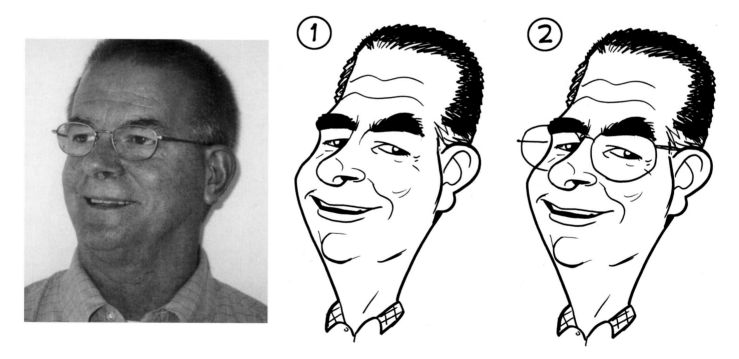

A very common thing for people with glasses to do is to take them off when they sit to be drawn. Most of the time this is a vanity issue, they think they look better without glasses. When this happens to me, I ask the model if they normally wear glasses. If they answer "hardly ever", then I'll drop the issue. If they say "always", I'll make sure they understand that if I draw them without the glasses, it'll look a lot less like them. I have to draw them how they normally look if it's going to look like them. Most of the time, but not always, they understand my point and put the glasses on again.

I even treat men's beards and mustaches as accessories (and the occasional woman's as well). Just like with glasses or bandages, I draw the likeness first, and then put in the add-ons, which in this case is the facial hair. Here's John for example:

① First I draw his face without the mustache:

② Then I add it on:

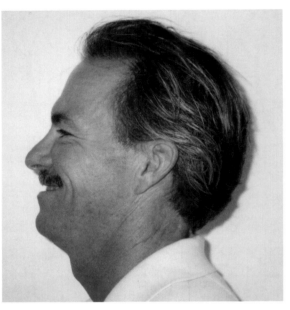

I drew Marc the same way, first clean-shaven, then with the facial hair. On a front view with facial hair, start in the center and draw out in the direction the hair actually grows!

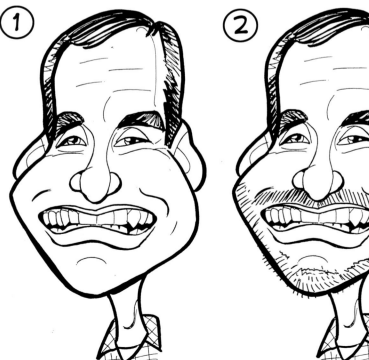

① ②

One of the most popular accessories to draw these days is a baseball cap. They can be tough to draw if you're not used to it, so let's go through it step by step:

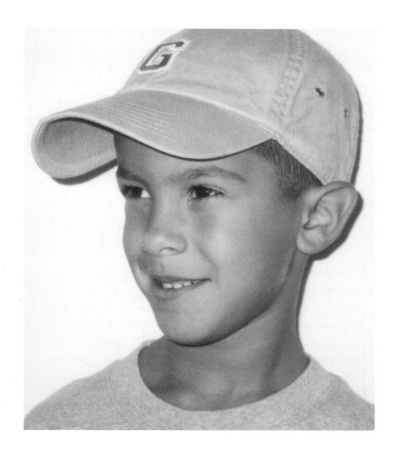

Face, ear and visible hair, leaving a blank space where the hat starts

Front underside of the cap's bill

The rest of the bill's underside

④

Top of the bill

⑤

Close off the bill, and continue the bottom line of the hat where it meets the ear

⑥

The shape of the rest of the hat

⑦

Fill in the rest of the visible hair and add detailing to the hat

In live caricaturing, I always try to have the model turn to a 3/4 view if they're wearing a baseball cap. However, whether it's because the model won't cooperate, or you have to draw from a full face photo only, sometimes you have to draw a cap from the front. I've chosen the full-face view of Mark to illustrate how I do it:

You'll notice I "cheated" the bill a little bit, showing more of it than is really visible in order to make the drawing easier to understand. If it makes your drawing stronger, don't be too tied down to reality!

77

BODIES

In caricatures, there's a long tradition of big heads and little bodies. My guess is that this is because it forces you to look at the face, which is the most important part. Also, it just looks funny. As you can see in these drawings, <u>how</u> big you make the head is up to you! You can draw them...

In my own work, I use the first proportion when I'm drawing a more conservative version of people. Number two is more like the exaggeration I use on most of my caricatures when I draw live. I also use number three sometimes when I draw live, but not as often, since it's more extreme. One advantage to it, however, is that it gives me lots of room in my drawing to play with the features of the face.

An important concept in drawing your caricatures is trying to get across your model's personality! Cary is an outgoing fellow with a positive outlook on life. He's the kind that never meets a stranger.

I've tried to get that attitude and personality across here by his open, "Here I am, world!" pose.

With Linzey Jr., you can tell by his confident smile and the way he holds his head, that he's a born leader:

So I try to get that attitude, that mood, across in his drawing:

Dominick is obviously mischievous. He seems to be plotting the next bit of trouble he can get into, doesn't he?

Speaking of trouble, Joan has three small boys, and they pull her in all directions. I went for an abstract swirl symbol for her eyes to give her the harried, dazed, overworked mom look. Notice also how even the untied shoes she's wearing reinforces this. It's as if all her time is spent taking care of her boys and there's none leftover for her to take care of herself. I got all of this across in one simple drawing.

Cartooning has such a rich visual language for you to use in order to get your points across like this. Learn to speak the language fluently and your caricatures will be infinitely better!

MEN'S HANDS

Most people have heard that hands are difficult to draw, and therefore they look at how an artist draws hands as part of judging how good the artist is...so don't "fake" your hands! Few things make a caricature look as amateurish as "rushed" or "sloppy" drawings of hands. When drawing men's hands I usually draw them with blocky fingers and bony knuckles.

Women's hands are usually smaller, and more graceful looking with thin, tapered fingers. Think grace and femininity as you draw them.

For years I kept sketchbooks that I would fill up with drawing after drawing of hands. I'd use my left hand as my "model", coming up with all sorts of poses, as my right hand drew.

The hands you draw can be fairly realistic, or very cartoony. On this page I've drawn for you some three-fingered cartoony hands, like you see on many classic cartoon characters.

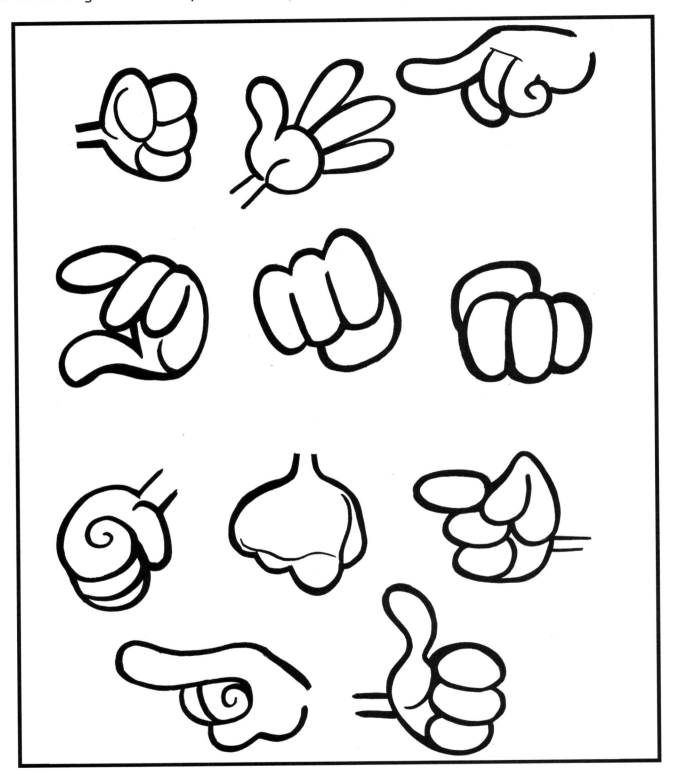

These kinds of hands can be really fun in a caricature. Think about it - three fingers just look funny! I also use some of these hands when drawing children, but I add the fourth finger back on them.

FEET

With men's feet, the bigger they are, the funnier they are, and the funnier, the better.

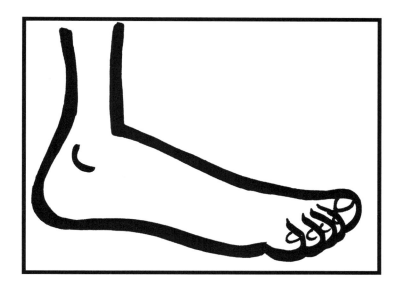

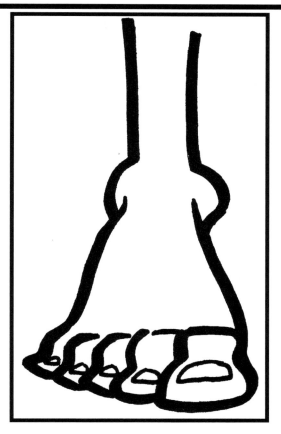

Big, funny, and hairy is even funnier!

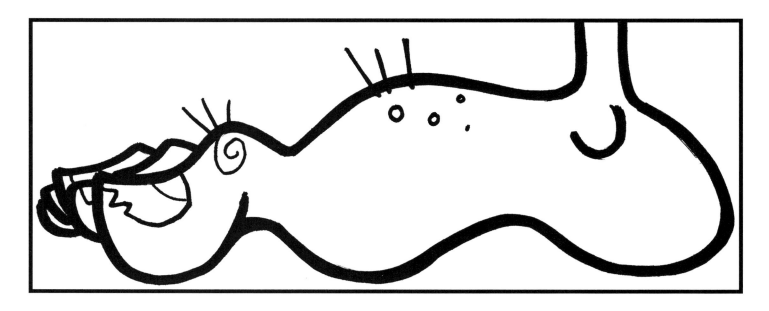

(Trust me - Don't put these on your female models...it won't go over well!)

With women's feet, make them smaller, daintier, and generally more feminine. I usually draw female feet very simple, without toes. Almost like a pair of dolls feet.

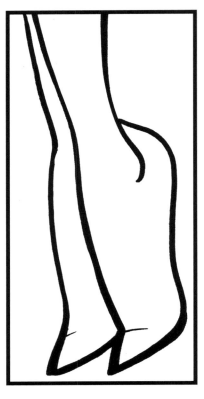

Small children's feet have little to no arch. Also, notice how high the foot is on top. This is due to a layer of fat there that children have and adults don't.

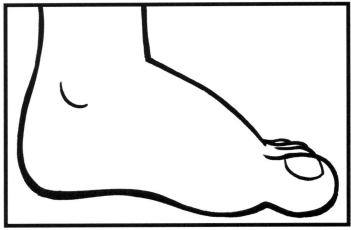

Of course, with most body situations you'll be drawing, you'll have to draw shoes rather than bare feet. Some artists' find shoes tough to draw, but I've always found them to be pretty easy, if you keep in mind the foot that's inside them. For example, with men and children, since their feet are larger in relation to their bodies, I draw the shoes large. With women, I draw the shoes small. An important thing when drawing shoes is to think of the simple shapes that they're made of, as with everything else in cartooning. Let's start with a simple one:

Notice the curves of these high-heeled ladies' shoes.

Another simple shoe to draw is the sports shoe with cleats. It's drawn with a simple wedge shape:

The "X" design makes good, simple shoelaces.

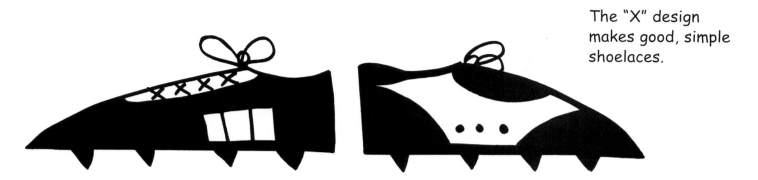

With athletic shoes, you've got unlimited choices as to which style to draw. I usually draw a variation of the old black and white high tops, just because I think they look funny and kind of cool. I also draw simple white tennis shoes when the pose calls for it.

This also shows another way I draw shoelaces.

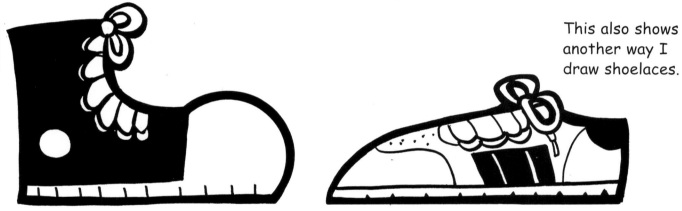

Finally, boots can be very complicated with their fancy heels, stitching, and other "extras". The important thing is to think simple shapes.

ACTION

For this concept, let's look at two lines:

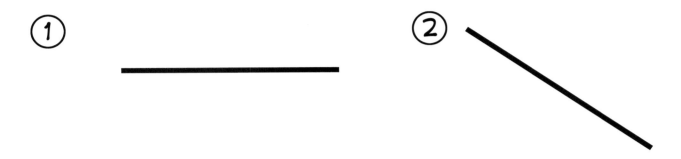

Which line is more interesting? Number two, right? Why? A diagonal line has more inherent "action" to it. The more diagonals in a picture, the more "action" it has, and that makes it more exciting to look at. Let's apply this to some figures:

Once again, number two has more action. See all of the diagonals in it?

Now let's put this "in action" on an actual caricature! Here's Linzey:

Notice all of the diagonals in the picture that I've pointed out for you.

I've made what could have been a boring pose exciting!

PENN'S
TIP:

DIAGONALS = ACTION
ACTION = ENERGY!

MEN

When I draw men, you'll notice I usually give them big hands and feet, and bony knees. Why? Because it's funny! I use a lot of the bowlegged poses like this one for the same reason. Here's Keith to illustrate:

Funny posture

Bony knees and bowed legs

Big hands and feet

In this picture of Steve...

I gave him a big upper body, emphasizing his masculinity, and skinny little legs:

This is a valuable cartooning concept that I use all the time called:
"VARYING PROPORTIONS".

It's a sure fire way to get a laugh with your drawings! Try it yourself - blow up the hands and leave the wrists tiny, blow up the feet and leave skinny ankles - there are endless combinations, and they're all funny!

91

On the following pages are what are known in live caricature as "gag bodies", or "body situations". You can use them to create a humorous picture of the model doing his or her favorite sport, hobby, or occupation. The situations I've included here are some of the most requested ones when I draw live.

Some situations, like this golf one, can be drawn very similar to other ones, such as baseball, on the next page.

Basic poses like this, "The Running Man", can be adapted to suit an endless amount of body situations!

92

Here you can see just a few of the body situations you can illustrate with this easy to learn pose:

Ideally, you should spend the majority of your time and effort in a live drawing getting a person's likeness, but don't skimp on the body!

This can be the most fun part of the picture!

WOMEN

Here's a photo of Kelly. She's a beautiful lady, so her caricature should reflect that. In fact, to emphasize her beauty even more, I've exaggerated some of her more feminine characteristics. I'll point them out for you.

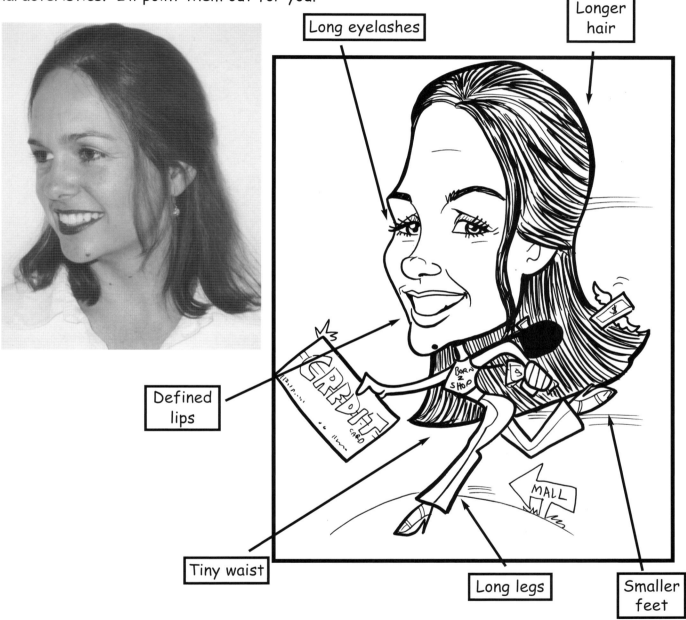

Long eyelashes

Longer hair

Defined lips

Tiny waist

Long legs

Smaller feet

Women come in all shapes and sizes, but what we're exaggerating here are the traits that are generally considered "more feminine". Just as I usually give guys larger hands and feet, and broader shoulders, because it's considered to be more masculine. In my drawings of women, like my drawings of children, I try to avoid any hard, angular lines when possible! The overall impression should be curves and softness.

95

Make your bodies age appropriate. As a daddy, I can tell you that no parent wants to see their little girl drawn with a pin-up girl body. I've seen a lot of artists make this mistake. I'll draw Brady here as an example of a good little girl body:

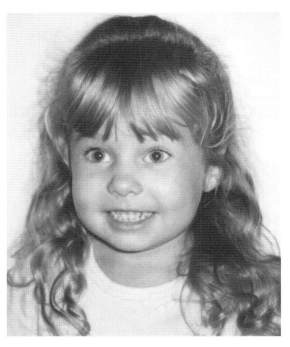

Since the model here is young, notice how I made her hands kind of large and "pudgier", using the cartoony hands I showed you. Notice again, how everything is about curves and softness. These kinds of things really do register subconsciously! Now let's look at how I took Doria and put her in an almost identical body situation. Except this body, when you compare, is definitely an adult's:

96

To further illustrate drawing age-appropriate bodies, here is a realistic teen body on Ally:

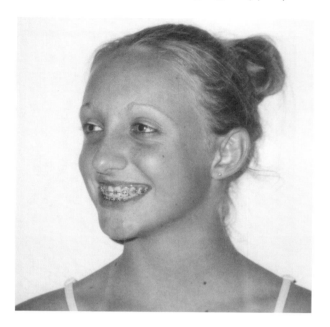

Contrasted with a grown up body on Lorie:

The bottom drawing has a more exaggerated body. I have more freedom as an artist to do this with adults. Remember, most of us would like to change at least some aspect of how we look, so flattery goes a long way when drawing caricatures! Most women like to be drawn with a body like the one above, just as most men like to be drawn as muscular "He-men". And if they're not really built that way, who cares? That makes it even funnier!

As I did with the guys, here are some body situations for you to use when drawing females (although most can be changed slightly and used for either).

Notice, in this drawing, how so many things; the length of the legs, the flowing hair, the tiny feet, all enhance the femininity of the pose!

This pose is also another variation on the "running man" pose! But the one leg pointed gracefully and the other kicked up behind looks more feminine.

These are two of the most popular poses for little girls:

While this computer whiz is popular for adults:

Notice here I've used the "Sitting Pose" - another of the endlessly adaptable poses I was talking about for you to practice and remember!

Here are some ideas for posing more than one person at a time together:

The most important question to ask here is, "Which person do you draw first?"

Being right handed, I always draw left to right, and continue that way even when drawing couples. With adults, I draw the guy first.

In a sibling picture, I use the "whoever takes up more space" rule to decide who sits and is drawn first. Usually this means the oldest goes first, but not always! All siblings, it seems, no matter what their age or race, fight with each other. Whenever I've used the pose to the right in a live caricaturing setting, it gets a big laugh.

In the case of similar sized models, like these friends, I don't have a preference of whom I start with. Whoever sits down first is the lucky one!

PENN'S TIP:

When drawing two or more people in a picture, have them sit separately and explain that you'll leave room for the 2nd person. This way you're able to concentrate on one face at a time! I've noticed if I have two people sit at the same time, they'll talk, kiss, or fight with each other, causing needless distraction.

So where did I get my ideas on seating order? Just like everything else, by experience. Early in my caricature career I was asked to draw a couple and the wife was going to sit first. Her husband had gone to buy her a drink, or something like that. I drew her, leaving space for her husband. Once hubby got there, I realized I had a big problem. The guy was a man-mountain! We're talking block-the-sun kind of big!

Boy, I sweated my way through that one! Half of the poor guy's head was covered up by his wife's hair, which she had no shortage of either. I immediately changed to drawing guys first, and it's worked much better. Let's face it, most of the time in a couple the guy is larger than the girl.

Here's a picture of Ryan and Marlee, as an example. They're fairly close in size, but Ryan is still a bit larger:

With Thomas and René, there's even a bigger size difference:

He's about a foot taller, and she has a lot of hair, so to draw her first would have been a real mistake!

For this picture, I took three separate photos and put them together for a cool abstract family caricature:

With adding a third person, my rules of placement change slightly. For this drawing, I drew the little boy, Reed, first. Then I drew his dad, John, and his mom, Wendy. Many times people think it is quicker, and should be cheaper, to include multiple faces in one drawing than to draw multiple drawings. Actually, the reverse is true. It's harder and often takes longer, because you have to be concerned with placement, and having enough room for all of the faces.

The more people you add in a drawing the more complicated it becomes. The ideal to me is one to three people, but I've drawn as many as one hundred people (with bodies) on an 11x14 drawing! For larger groups I suggest the following configurations (I've numbered the heads in the order I draw them):

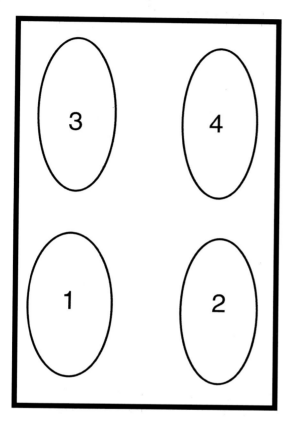 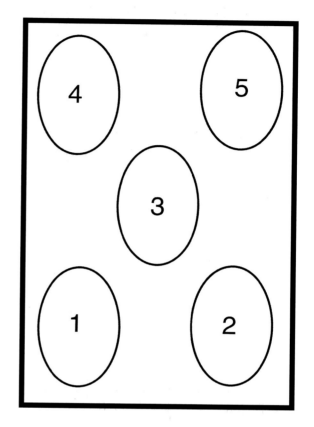

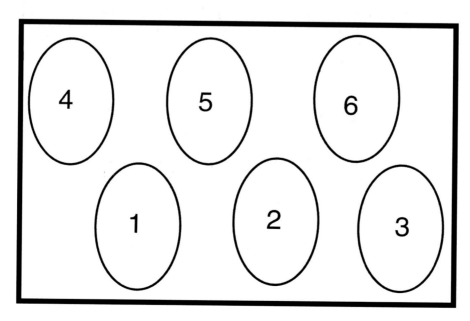

BACKGROUNDS

Backgrounds are immensely important to a good face and body caricature, but they should complement the rest of the picture, not overpower it. With this drawing of Mistie, I've pointed out some background tips:

Simple "scalloped" clouds break up the white space around the figure.

A cartoony spectator adds another level of depth and a touch of humor!

Keep a low ground line in your drawings. Remember, the less ground you draw, the less you have to color! It also helps "frame" the figure.

Never underestimate the power of silhouette (blacked in) shapes. They help set the scene, but don't detract from it.

SILHOUETTES

Silhouetted (blacked out) shapes, like the cityscape in the previous picture, are great for backgrounds and "props" like trees, goalposts, etc. Remember how I said earlier "when in doubt, leave it out"? I've got another saying for you that rhymes with that one. The new one goes "when in doubt, <u>black</u> it out!" If you can't draw something, say a gun, draw the basic shape in black. If it looks like a gun, it is a gun! Besides being quick and easy to draw, the black gives some contrast to the picture.

LETTERING

The most important lettering you'll do on a caricature is your model's name. Shouldn't you be able to tell whom the drawing is of without the name? Yes. But most people just like to have their name on their caricature. My advice to you about names is to write the name first!

I'll never forget a few years ago when I drew a picture something like this:

THEN I found out the kid's name was "Maximillian". I didn't have room to fit that name, and of course Mom and Dad wouldn't hear of me writing just "Max". Yikes! I learned...write the name first! To this day, I affectionately refer to this as the "Maximillian Rule".

Over the years, I've seen artists do many types of lettering for names, and I've tried most of them myself. The one I've found to be the most popular is "balloon lettering". There are many variations, but mine looks like this:

You may notice that I kind of "squash" my letters together...

So instead of:

NAME

I write:

NAME

A LOT OF THIS IS PERSONAL PREFERENCE, BECAUSE I JUST THINK IT LOOKS COOLER. IT ALSO TAKES UP LESS SPACE, SO YOU CAN DRAW MORE, AND IT LETS YOU WRITE LONGER NAMES. PLUS, IF YOU COLOR, IT'S EASIER BECAUSE YOU DON'T HAVE TO WORRY ABOUT COLORING OUT OF THE LINES!

LINES

A good caricature is about exaggeration and likeness. Good line quality WON'T make your caricatures better, but it will make them **LOOK** better!

Smooth, clean lines, like these I've drawn Bob with are more appealing to the eye. They give the drawing a sense of confidence.

Also, notice again, that my outside lines are thicker than my inside ones. This gives a sense of depth by having everything in the background drawn with thinner lines. This is a helpful technique I've used on most of the pictures in this book!

PENN'S TIP:

When you're using a marker, it's easier to make a smooth line when you draw quickly, than if you draw slowly. If you draw slowly, your pen has more time to bleed. So, "see" your line on the page before you draw it, then put it down quickly!

A good way to draw smooth and clean is to draw "down strokes" with your pen, like this:

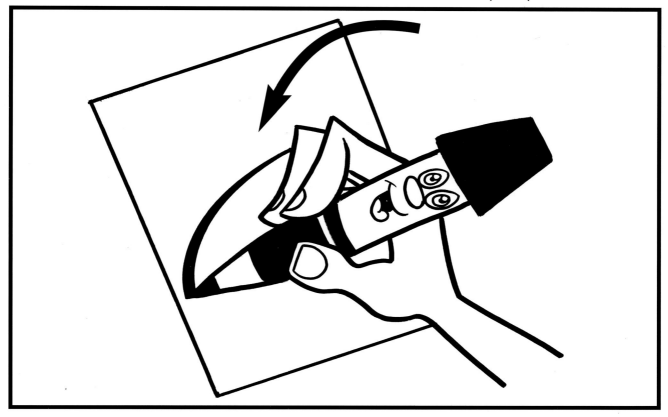

It is much more difficult to draw smooth lines when you make "up strokes". Give it a try!

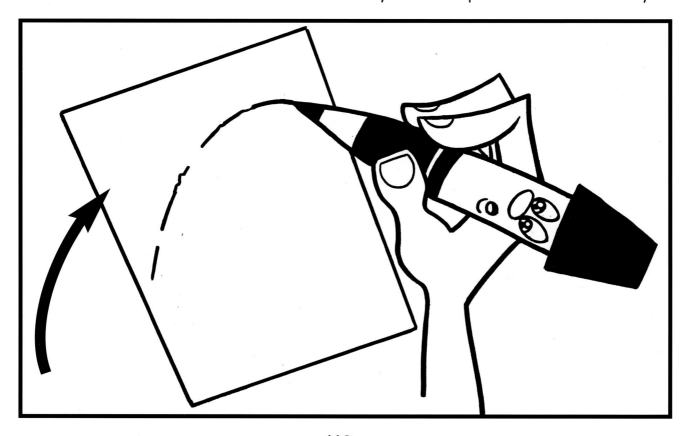

DON'T DRAW...

Vanity sometimes gets the best of us all. Often your models will try to control how they look in your caricature of them by offering you advice. It usually starts with "Don't Draw..."

...Or as I like to put it, "Make me twenty years younger, twenty pounds lighter and make it look just like me!" Uh...yeah...right! As a caricature artist, you have to face it (pun intended) - people are insecure about their looks. But aren't we all, to some degree?

Be honest with yourself, there's probably a feature or two of your own that you'd rather people overlook or, at the very least, didn't magnify too much!

Still, the simple fact of the matter is, if you're going to make the drawing look like your subject, you have to draw what is there...or at least make it **LOOK** like you did! Confused?

Which drawing do you think this boy will like the best? This one...

...Or this one?

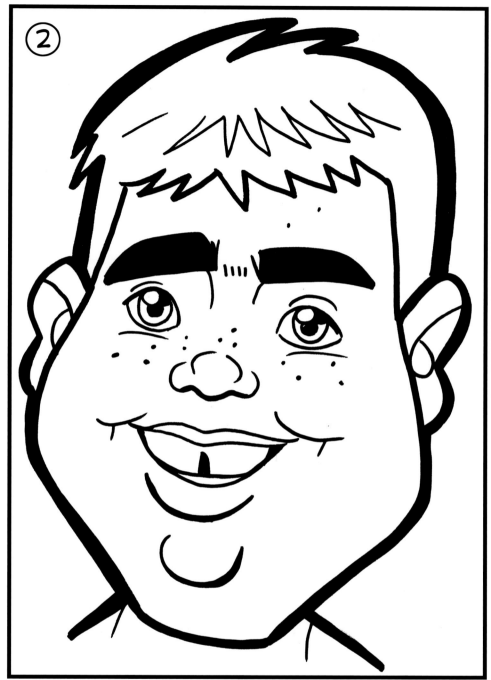

You picked the second one, right? It still shows the boy is overweight, has freckles, a split between his teeth and hair between his eyebrows. However, it's much kinder. I used my "nice pen" on him. Don't misunderstand me; I'm not saying to do this with everyone's drawings! Some people can handle honesty and exaggeration, and some can't.

It is up to you to be the judge of this. When in doubt though, be nice! Since live caricatures are usually done in a retail/party environment, pleasing the customer/guest is your number one concern. In this setting, if the customer doesn't like the drawing, it's really not a good caricature. No matter how great it is actually drawn!

PEOPLE TO LOOK OUT FOR

When drawing caricatures live, you'll eventually come in contact with all three of the categories of people I'm about to discuss with you. We'll talk about each so you know how to handle them. Let's start with...

MOVING TARGETS

Whether they're one, or one hundred and one, they can't seem to sit still. Always moving, always talking, they can be a real challenge. My advice? Breathe deeply and just be patient! You can always use a pencil if you need to - so you can erase. The real key is to give them a <u>focal point</u>. Whether it's a member of their family, or a spot on the wall, giving them something to look at will help keep them still. I've also known caricaturists who would wear silly hats, talk in silly voices, or wear puppets on their non-drawing hand to get a model's attention. Those gimmicks aren't my style personally, but they may work for you so try them if you'd like!

The next type we come to is:

BEAUTIFUL
PEOPLE
(OR THOSE WHO
THINK THEY ARE)

Keep in mind that what you're dealing with here is a vanity issue, and vanity is insecurity in disguise. Just humor a model that is like this and tell them you'll use your "nice pen" on them. It's interesting to me that truly beautiful people are usually the least vain. It's the ones who deep down know they're not beautiful, but act like they are, that can cause problems for the artist drawing them.

Finally, we come to my least favorite:

THE HECKLER

SHE DOESN'T HAVE A MUSTACHE!

OH MY GOSH! WAIT TILL YOU SEE WHAT HE DID TO YOU!

HEY, YOU GAVE HIM THREE EYES!

Yes, they're being rude. And no, they're not being funny. But really, they think they are. The best response is no response. When they don't get a laugh, they'll usually go away. If they don't and are unusually persistent, I turn the joke on them by drawing an unflattering caricature of them into the picture I'm currently drawing. It never fails that they quit heckling when they realize the joke is now on them!

PENN'S TIP:

Hecklers usually won't say anything about a truly bad picture. They'll just walk away. So in a way, having a heckler is weird sort of compliment. At least he's watching - you must be doing something right!

Now let's put everything we've learned together in some drawings:

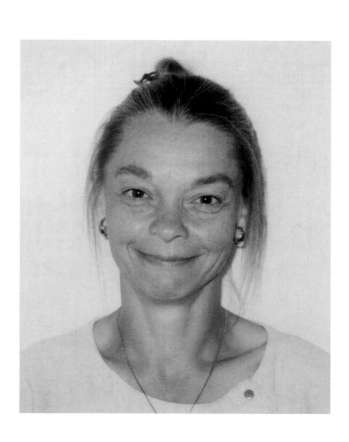

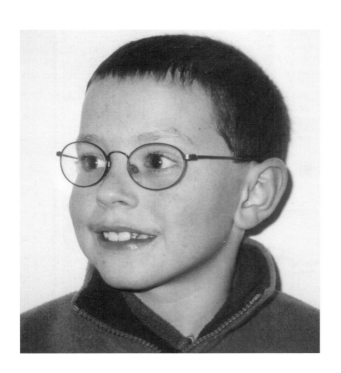

Okay, now you're on your own! Throughout this book, you've been able to look at my renditions of the photos as you've been practicing. But no help on these! Use what you've learned, and see what YOU come up with!

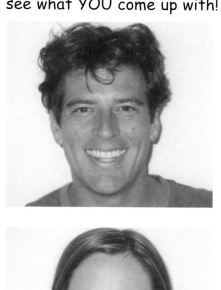

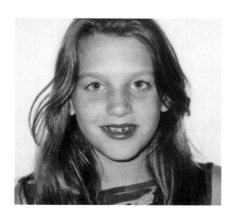
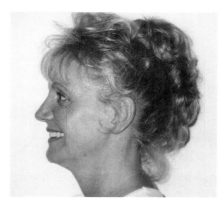
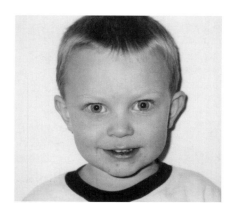

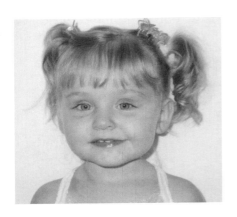  

127

INDEX